Glossary of Unsaid Terms

About Chad Walsh

The Chad Walsh Chapbook Series is supported by Alison Walsh Sackett and her husband, Paul, in honor of Ms. Sackett's father, Chad Walsh (1914-1991), a cofounder in 1950 of the *Beloit Poetry Journal*. An author and scholar, Walsh wrote several books on literary history, including *The End of Nature* and *Hang Me Up My Begging Bowl*. He was professor and writer-in-residence at Beloit College in Wisconsin for thirty-two years, serving for many of those years as chair of the English Department. He also taught as a Fulbright lecturer in Finland and Italy.

Other Books in the Series

In the Time of PrEP
Jacques J. Rancourt

The Wanderer
Christine Gosnay

Glossary of Unsaid Terms
Victoria C. Flanagan

The Chad Walsh Chapbook Series
Beloit Poetry Journal, Gorham, Maine

Cover design: Seth Pennington
Cover art: Head, neck, shoulder and chest of a dissected male
écorché, with arteries and blood vessels indicated in red. Coloured
lithograph by J. Roux, 1822. Wellcome Collection. Attribution 4.0
International (CC BY 4.0)
Interior design: Melissa Crowe
Editors: Melissa Crowe and Jessica Jacobs

Permissions:
Beloit Poetry Journal
P.O. Box 1450
Windham, ME 04062
bpj@bpj.org
www.bpj.org

ISBN: 978-1-7320411-2-7

Contents

Self-Portrait as My Mother Would Have It

Hair curled just so, and not the kind of woman
to up and shun the Blue Ridge,
Fred's Mercantile, the fawns that crept
over Beech's dry October slopes,
or the turn-season glory of flame azalea,
black gum, sugar maple, Table Mountain pine.
She speaks soft, wears her grandmothers' charms
and calls them armor—Margie's pearls
and Nora Mae's ruby—and she can key through
the hymnal by rote. She, who did exist
for a moment, never wandered, never left
dishes to dry in the rack. She never walked out
to see her father killing feral cats—
a backroad, two-step death: crushed
throat and a Buck knife—and never dosed out
the week in a back bathroom, water running
over the crack-open of scrip-orange lids,
white-tablet rattle on laminate. No, she inherited
only that which is good. No craving
for the highway out of town, for dope bags slung
under the Boyd Bridge that stitches
the Carolinas together. Her only testament
is that of the Piedmont's late-bloom
honeysuckle. Watauga's whitewater, the snap
of a male cardinal lifting from a snow-lit branch. Grown,
this woman knows decency doesn't depend
on ending consonants, tracks planting seasons
by the height of pigweed in blind Harvey's pasture.
She's *good-china* delicate. Her mother's devotion
a garland upon her brow. Faithful, she knows
winter pays up in the magnolia's swell,
bloom, and seed-drop, and she remembers
what her grandfather quoted about fear:
*Out here, any watchman keeps awake
in vain.* She can rattle off the six creeks flowing
out of Valle Crucis, and nothing has been taken
from her, especially not by force. No switchblade,
no *just relax.* She has no reason
to apologize. And though she chooses, always, to stay,
she knows how long it takes to get way out,

past the ridgeline—God's Damascus blade
before the afterlife, it must be, as it always
has been. She trusts in this, still.

In the Operating Room

I'm kept awake, watching
a body caught in its revolt.

All this began, as you'd expect, simply:
a phone call, ceremony

of diagnosis, a confluence of details
spanning some rift between lived

and heard,   but it also began

two appointments prior:
the slicing of skin, dermatologist's biopsy

a fresh, desperate probing. On the receiving end
of the doctor's careless dial, my mother

picked up and said, *You might as well
tell me,* and so she goes on knowing my body

before I know it.
          Then, a week later, my surgeon

won't stop quoting Frost, griping
about his youngest son over my incisions,

extracting cancerous obelisks from my shin, each
the size of a thumbprint. Earlier, his questions:

*These cells are not like the other cells—do you know
why such things happen?*

          I thought I knew, thought this rampancy
had only to do with wasting away—generic

and aged: a great uncle, an elder deacon,
the constant ebb of well-meant takeout trays

hitting the trash can full, grandmother
unhungered, beloved but nothing more

than a sigh upon entering a room
when chemo took her stomach lining, too.

       Can I comprehend
this violence,

watching blood pool before
the stitch?   I assumed the body was fated

for mutiny. But not this
quick.   Will I always

fear, now, baring this skin
to light? I do not think of myself

telling my children, someday,
as my father had to, that this was simply the start

of a long road into wilderness, the inevitability
of bloodline and bad luck.

The surgeon stitches a solid line of blue
where the blot had been.   Maybe this

is the first of a hundred malignancies
and maybe someday they will take

everything, all of me, stitch me back together apart
from my self, this self that had known so well

other fears and panics and herself.

And in post-op, when a nurse outlines recovery time, I'll say
I hope September turns cold, that I want to hide away

like the year I fled up North for breathing room, and maybe
I'll convince someone after all: *there is more to me*

even now that I have been made less,   lesser.

    What am I, if not the body?

Like an offering, I bare
the memory of a well self

to the surgical lamp—split skin seamed
into a garrison of scars, dark

as cherries.

Girl with Game Boy

Growing up, I toured radiation clinics
every few months, made the doomsday visit

each time the doctors said Nora Mae
was close. Bright machines, lead vests, kid-friendly
proof of fact, billed as a grief group
for "cancer families." To see is to believe:

months, years here, and nothing
could have saved her. Stooped men in gowns
shuffled wide halls, lost boys pulled toward LINAC,
tomo-, while a counselor, once more, explained cancer

is *the body   killing   the body.*   My father'd quiz me
all the way home   *What did you learn?*
and I wouldn't sleep for days. Left-right, A-B
till dawn, ticking frogs across a pixeled river—

no, not so much has changed.   I've stretched to six feet
but still sit knees to chest.   I wait to be called,
should be reading, answering emails, not darting
this tweaked-out hedgehog across a screen, ticking

a d-pad through the months: four becomes seven, eight,
twelve. Each gamesave adds to guilt:
I should've made a record,
          I should have something to say
about bad lobby art, the office lights' flicker, my two-a-days

of total-body radiation.   First visit, my doctor said
Being sick takes practice. He promised
You'll learn.   But here, for now
I'm the young gun—best-case kid—brave one,

and when other patients pass by they say   *Honey,*
you'll grow old   like a rite or a dismissal. Like they mean it.

When a Nurse Reminds Me That Exhaustion
Is the Primary Side Effect of Treatment

　　Each high-output fluorescent
is a tambourine, a clattering,
　　a drop-ceilinged coda. No—

each high-output fluorescent
　　is the opposite of hyacinth or maybe,
each high-output fluorescent

is a no-shit moment, vitreous
　　and bright-blind, a crisis

of alchemy. I cannot look

at Lucy's face as she wipes the blood
　　and bile from my lips, second time
this round. I stare instead

at my scabbed palm's
　　head line, the only gentle thing in sight.

There are, I imagine, nearly infinite experiences

　　of remoteness. The usual separations, surely,
make an appearance:　　time and place,
　　detachment, destination-based finales,　　expirations.

The average high-output fluorescent
　　has a 24,000-hour lifespan, its barrage
of lumens bright white,

or cool white, or neutral.

　　And yet, and yet,
because everything that begins
　　ends, and because all matter

must traverse some distance,
   here, too, incremental—
starts and stops between

starting and stopping—all this waiting,

these   you've-got-a-ways-to-go-befores,
   teach us to measure,   to mark.

   I was told to expect four rounds
five rounds back.

   Stagnation is a new hostility,
a cicatrix splitting open. *Sit up,* she says.

      Sit up.

This fundamental—perhaps personal—
   failing of the body. Which is to say nothing
of incremental distances,   becoming—

Because *improvement* and *advancement*
   are synonyms. Because *improvement*
and *expansion, improvement* and *enlargement* are not. Because

improvement means *to become well again,*
      returning

to a body I'd never pick out
   in a lineup as mine—

   sallow, sharp-boned, starved
   for light—

   and a gray
is one joule of radiation per kilo
   of matter. Gray is *intermediary,*

dose, is *emissary.* Gray is a dilution
   of standard treatment, compromise to keep you
working, working to keep you

insured. Gray is the pain-med substitute.
Gray is the question *Have I done this*
   to myself?

   It is an open gown
in a muted color. Gray is not grief itself.

                                   ■

Lucy says I look better these days
   and I wonder how we measure progress
without admitting bias. *Don't forget*

that this will end, Vic.

   What is *target*,

   aim, or *end* if not
a subjectivity? A finish line
       is also a division. What is it

        I am *becoming?*

If I blink even once,
   I will fall immediately into sleep.

Not a week ago, I watched a tidal creek

fill and swell from dry-bed nothing—
   a kind of benediction
before the cycle

began again.   I stared out

and out toward the drowned cordgrass,
       stock-still, expectant.

In Response to My Mother When She Says
Hearing Me Read My Writing's Like Hearing God

In my world, God is a crystalline superstructure, God
    is a molecular bond. God is the space, Mother,
between Fibonacci's one and one. God is not my

    word for good days—it is yours—and so *God*
really makes no appearance. Exiled from all my
    early drafts, my rationales: Mother,

I wasn't sure how to tell you. How to tell—the truth is, Mother,
    that all those would-be-honeyed prayers I whispered up to God
became the grotesque stories of a sleepless child, my

    Sunday teachings warped to torture. Mother,
Ruth and Athalia fought to the death for God's
    favor in my dreams, and neither won. When my

Sunday school teacher—Paul?—went to jail for molesting my
    peers, when those five men in four years forgot all their mothers
never taught them—seams pressed into me in an alley, a hallway,
    a field out toward God

    knows where, right there in my bedroom, upstairs, right there—
    tell me, why does God
let policemen fuck—yes, I say *fuck* now, Mother—
    women in their custody? Mother, it is legal in 32 states,
    and my God,

South Carolina is one of them. Don't ask, Mother, how I
    know. Know that when I speak, my
words are mine. You can call it bitterness, vanity,
    but it is only proof of my
ability to care for myself, to begin again. Because when you
    were grieving, Mother,

    the type of pearl-clad woman I would never be, I tended
blotched, cancerous skin, a three-centimeter mass in my chest: God,
    what of that? What of what I have become? I had all the God

you'd given me, and I've sat in fourteen hospital chapels, God
    still a no-show. God is a no-show. God, as you exalted him, saw my
MRIs, blood counts, and said *This, give her this, too,* but why, God,

do I feel that I should give thanks, stage communion with my
every effort—I can't write around the rhythms, this mother
    tongue of the place I ran from. I'm a made thing,
        and it's language—Mother,

this is where we meet. How could you hear me read aloud
        and not remember a mother's
    covenant: birthed silent and blue, I refused to breathe for weeks.
        God heard and God
produced a debt: firstborn's life against all odds. I don't know
        what promises, Mother,

    you made. I am grateful, I'm grateful, it is just—they say the body
        remembers, my
body must remember how to fight, pluck must linger in the blood,
        haunt my
    white counts. Yes, it must be the numbers. It has to be
        in the numbers. God

cannot be remission, the clear scan, a bell's clang after my
    last treatment. God cannot be needle, drip bag, R-CHOP,
God cannot be the clot I throw, the fourteen God-forsaken

    calls I almost made from the waiting room, wanting
to tell you, Mother, this—which I will not read to you
    I am sick again, and I am sorry. Mother, I know

I'm not the daughter you want. I just wasn't sure
    how to say it,

Caeneus Struck by Side Effects
at a Late-Night 7-Eleven

*In her youth, the maiden Caenis was captured and raped by Poseidon,
who then promised to grant her any wish she could name. Without
hesitation, she asked to be made a man so she would not be raped again.
Poseidon bestowed upon the renamed Caeneus both manhood and
invincibility, guaranteeing that no human weaponry could pierce the
warrior's skin in battle. While some accounts claim Fate returned Caeneus
to female form later in life, most avow he died a man, defeated by his
enemies only when buried under a great weight and suffocated in the earth.*

Between retches, I study the frosted window to my right
as if for the first time: etching

sallow, nicked and private. I'll look anywhere
but down. Here, on the tile floor of a pit stop,

I divide my loneliness into parts. Section off
the havebeen agonies, the stillare

regrets, lace-delicate: just weeks into gestation,
my radiated body rejects

what it might not bear. No, my body is not a vessel,
it is a canyon, particle ricochet rising to the edge,

DNA split, each invalid afternoon
a mortal souvenir.   But why

attend this constant vigil
for myself?   No one says *buck up*

to the faithless. Anointed by bleach
& a testosterone patch, I imagine a mammoth skull

dug up & drug through midtown. A crowd
stares on as the crane hoists, the tusks

make miniatures of us all. Asphalt buckles
mile after mile, baring in noon light the century's graves.

It's not fair to say *excising*
when it may have been *unearthing,*

uncovering, discovering—strangeness
evolves by degrees: I was dug up spitting

red clay, voice choked down
an octave from silt.   But I have proven,

time & again, unfit. Inviable. Each biopsy
sews up a question—this body not quite *danger,* not quite

deathtrap.   Is it that my body, if it could bear
would bare a thing incomplete   *as girl?*

But uncertainty is not a menace
in itself. Over the sink I remind myself, *take heart:*

A window is not a mirror, and who am I, anyway,
to disrupt the wonder of all this   revision?

Vox Populi, Vox Dei

My father taught me well: you can split whole cords
with a chipped maul & still forsake

the shed. Proof: corner store ruptured
by weeds chin-high, even the high school

has closed. Out here, where tire plants landmark,
mill men drift and jaw:

If you cut both a man's hands from his body,
even his family will think him dead.

    Father, debtor, crankhead, snitch.

       No one revenge
will do—*harm* has a hectare

of timberwoods & a zip code
where people say belief

is what gets them through.
To be *girl* in a place where bruise

is prelude. We all learn quick
as a clip point blade—cool and nicking

threat against the inner thigh.

      My father taught me well:
Can't chase away a name. This is the earth

I shall inherit: Steam idles over
the recycling plant, slack bales queue up

in these, our dry fields, & his bones
won't thaw before March.

Out here, you ask a man for mercy
he'll spit and call you senseless.

You tell this land *Forget me*
but it gives you sons instead.

Foo Dog To Go, Between Rounds

Richmond, VA

I.

Dusk in March and every shadow's doubled
by streetlights, long stretch

of limb, body smooth and tossed aside. Profile
creased to line drawing, I jaywalk

for takeout. Curried rice noodles, gyoza
with stripe of hot sauce: pity dinner.

Diagnosis makes *before*, makes *since then*,
writes its timeline. I've been told I should expect

extremes, quick switches, swings—
the hormones' side effects. I'm right on schedule.

To swing is to sway, to change
drastically —a coup or a landslide

or a late-game substitution,
my noradrenaline Hail Mary—

this dark parabola. Every now and then
I miss the upside, hypomania squandered

for restless mornings
with someone I love, trying

to convince myself to relish,
that there's no writable reason to work

seventeen hours, to run twelve miles,
to scrub the stove, to bleach the sink

or pace the room and dread
the airport drop-off

when I'll watch him walk away,
because he will walk away:

She probably can't have kids, but there's hope
with hormones that maybe,

years from now, who knows.

He must have thought
I was out of earshot, primping

down the hall when he said it—
leaving and parting, I know,

are not the same.

I couldn't help but wonder,
feeding my parking stub into a kiosk,

if it was the last time he'd see me.
I had not told him my doctor called

to follow up—routine scans
inconclusive. I know what it means

when they need more blood, I know
what happens next.

                    To rise
only as far as gravity permits—

To return mercifully
and inevitably to center—

I give my name to the hostess
guarding the brown bags.

The window's neon Foo dogs
hawk good luck to the college students

stumbling by. I must eat regular meals. Must
sleep and know this curse

is biotic, not him and not
absence, know it would have come

either way, this neurochemical
bottoming out just

as inevitable—
I swallowed hormones for months,

the doctor called it *preservation,*
that I may one day bear a new

and healthy body into the world,
some kind of blessed erasure.

But I refused to doubt my chest swelling past
side effect, past waiting-room platitude, past

this too shall stop happening
to you, *this too shall* never reappear.

As if I could will it, as if my chest
weren't now far-off and foreign,

as if my body remained
both a victory and my own.

I bought binders, reminded myself
You are living, then two dense spots

on the CT, one in each breast—
they could be called inevitable, too.

Second cancer tempting third,
casualty of two-a-days

in a radiation clinic: benign masses,
close calls. For weeks

I buttoned my shirts
bottom to top, shaking.

II.

                    To traverse,
to aspire. To swing: make a fist,
rear back and crack bone,

let the ego speak—I'd prefer *just the way it goes*
over *taken from us,* over *such a shame.*

Quit the highs and lows and live—
not *brave,* not *brilliant,*

I am spectacle, inevitable body—
what else can I do?

Time and again I have been lucky. I Google
preventative top surgery, top surgery

cancer prevention?   Waiting for my order,
I Google *top surgery v double mastectomy*

scars, I Google *top surgery*
paid for by health insurance, then *top surgery*

psychological aftermath.

No. Speak plain:
I am too terrified or lonely

or arrogant or vain to knife off
what could kill me,

what would testify,
attest publicly, prove

that I have not come through
unscathed, that every certainty

I've ever had has fled. I know this body,
which so often speaks for me,

will not be spoken for. Will I
get to make

a choice at all?

I spent five nights
not saying and he left.

Maybe he said it so I would hear,
maybe he understood:

years from now, who knows.
    What would I give

to know I've made it through,
that it will all be over soon?

I pay and tip—
the hostess thanks me twice—

then retrace the five blocks home,
twine-handled bag heavy,

a feat, a pendulum
keeping time.

What would I do
to be rid of it all,

what would I do
to see thirty?

Rough Draft as Caeneus Abroad

Grant I might not be a woman: you will have given me everything.
—Caenis to Poseidon, *Metamorphoses,* Book XII

*He did not understand that there is as much liberty and latitude in the
interpretation as in the making...*
—Montaigne

I.

I have this theory: everything I've written
is really an acquisition

of language   or acquisition
    of one language over another.

Like when I watch skiers laze down
Snoqualmie's slope   like melt,

like Kees's bathers
stuck in the wrong season. Or the way

    a former student writes me to say
she's *experienced a traumatic event*

& my hands stiffen & begin to ache
on instinct.   *How do we make sense*

of tragedy in writing? she asks me
over iced coffee, expecting

I know.   A steamer wand screams
into milk, a muffin cools on a blue plate—

she was the first neighbor to respond
to the father's yell & she is shaken.

The real question:
what is the poetic voice in excess of?

        I am three thousand miles from the place

that made me. Now
in a place with a windy season,

a fire season,
brim of the high desert,

I can see scorched earth & whitecaps
from the same June lookout.

That which takes us captive
shapes us, too. Out here

no Poseidon ever makes good: I'm refused

service at the brewery off 3rd
in my oversized clothes, & an ex says

   Stop being dramatic
over FaceTime when I remind him: *not she,*

& suddenly I've become
a *your kind* with no kin to call on

& missionaries begin to find my doorstep
twice a week. Who is there,

in this place, to grant me
release?

  The dirt-floor arena waits

below a bluff, empty
fifty weeks a year, & I watch the day sink,

thinking *Ravisher, make me anew*
in the shadow of high mountains, grant me

liminal-unthinkable, take this,
all of this besides—

& that body, released
  dismissed discarded might

become mine.

      When she first wrote me,
the student closed her request to meet

In the real world I'd like to think
we would have been friends.

    Real's a whole affair, you see,
so little space for those

you cannot name for certain, but it matters
what you celebrate in a thing, too:

   Name me a god
who hasn't thundered.   That one may speak

& be heard becomes a demand
    to speak and be heard.

II.

My student tells me that a father
    backed over his daughter with his pickup.
She died chest-split, staining the grass black.

My student talks about the hush
    that smothers a block

even weeks later.

The mind, tethered
    to the body, officiates
our mythmaking. Surveillance buffs

mythos from physical container—
    the body is nothing
but a marionette. In my head,

I've got hellhounds
    on a pack lead
strutting down Pine:

all transition is violence,
     erosion, & origin at once—two mirrors
facing out from opposite walls—cause

          & invention.

I try to search up the name
          of the child—

accident father death girl Seattle,
     pickup truck neighborhood accidental death—
but come up empty. Name me

a god who hasn't plundered.

Tragedy & spectacle:
          these twin puncture wounds.

III.

Cast out, I begin each day with an invocation
for what I've lost, passing:

Let my captors have the legend
if I may keep the sound which marks

my life like a bell.

The quarter I'd had this student
I shaved my head for the first time:

homemade undercut, radiation carryover.
Two years since the scare of a tumor

in my chest, the body bears the mark
of every way it's been:

I look tough and tired.
This tradition

of the Narcissian pool
obligates a final reflection—

Chase down the name

so that we can have power over it,
draw the force of the thing right up to us—

& so I swallow hard when my student admits
she Googled my name, a name

that is no longer enough.   I cannot tell her
that every Thursday for all those weeks,

classes let out to the sweep
of a weekend, I drove the canyon road south of campus

with my lights off, I took every rock-wall turn
last-second swearing, sometimes,

   I never touched the wheel at all.

IV.

Rebel Poseidon, defiler
of the genderedbody, wield
your sharpest knives. Cut away,
take & remake in the image

of what you fear most. Avenge
your boundary with doubt,
all those titles which never fit:
necessity of reinvention   a hard year

fleeting emotional response   this container with its own rules.
Name me a god who hasn't pardoned
and cursed in the same breath.
Every idea is a question, too,

& my top surgery is denied
a third time—too risky amid the body's constant
sway between well & ill—
& I tell myself *Never mind.* I tell myself

You are seeking comfort
in a body incapable of such things. Some days
I tell myself *There is nothing*
to be done. There is so much work

to *becoming.*

V.

When the buzz grew back
& decisions had to be made,

I tried *boy*. Hair pulled tight, smoothed
to one side, I thought *yes*, body as

boy, which became *boi*, then *then*,
then *was*, then *just maybe*, then just *vessel*, then

nothing more, then *just this once*, then
neveragain.

Thing is, we don't have canyons where I'm from,
just the junk of melt and migration:

passivity, inevitable landscapes. Appalachia
is all slow creep. But ridges—

the exposed rock of a canyon wall
is what remains

when a river has bored its way through.
Name me a god without design.

I have learned to take, too.
My night drive carved its shape

from red desert and basalt,
riparian zone: the surrounding biome

of this foreign earth, a strip of habitat
between the river & the land beyond.

An interplay,
a margin: Space to remake,

right and revise
the narrative—cell mutation, bones hollowed,

chest cracked open like a seed
in surgical—I deadname

girl   belle   proper
frailmeekthing   deadname

diagnosis   relapse and recur. Instead take up
them, of consequence, reluctant then *a made thing,*

then *threat,* then *body between.*
Is the line not so very thin

between making again   & making new?
Galvanized, then *forged, rewarded*

for a long and searching gaze.   Taking
& taking up,   armed—

I have acquired. Name me the god
who says *Yes, and.*

Worthy animal.
I have learned

all sacrament rests on the tongue.

Prayer for the Self on I-24 W

Most days you dream of your native switchbacks,
hairpins, climb and low-gear return—the inevitable

reappearance *in town,* as they say. Those state roads
the province of your grandfather's haunting, his totems

a spectral suite: Haggard cassettes, gliding silver Buick,
NC plate stamped 5OCLOCK. Nostalgia is easy enough.

But this highway is straight and strange. Twenty-four years
and this the one time you've struck out on a whim? The first *I-guess*

acquiescence to a 24-hour jaunt. Is it only when we go west
that we ask ourselves who we are?

In the lead car ahead, your friend doesn't know —
your own coughs having woken you—that you did feel, did want her

hand on the small of your back, palm impulsive in near-sleep.
Because you stayed silent and still. This denial, typical—you chase

down the recital of an old self. Eighty miles from Nashville, this road
is an arrival, a paying up. What would be blessed, if you allowed it:

to list misstep without caveat, call callousness
and fuckups by their names. Caeneus reshrouded

as woman, right yourself and live what you have earned.
When the time is right, petition the rift between

backwoods beginnings and a red-lipped profile
picture. Say it aloud so that you yourself may hear: *God the Father*

*of my obligations, let me trust my mongrel tongue. Give me
strength to speak, to risk, and let me not be only that*

which raised me. Feet to flame, admit: *I have frightened myself
into cruelty.* This, above all, is true.

Poem for Lactic Acid

I.

I didn't call it foreshadowing then—radial shatter
    a month before the first mass,
stranger's bat taken to my windshield.
I walked out one morning for a run

and ran my hand over splintered glass,
    not thinking. I'd never touched
    a shattered thing. Blood rose
through my skin in wild lines,

pooled dark. The morning I see *NED*
    on a laser-printed page—type
    clear as excision, clean
as pathology report, MRI unmarred

and unmistakable—I run seventeen miles
    without noticing. Out in the cold, choir
    of silver moons tracking sky—

                This is not to say
everything becomes, suddenly, lovely.

My foot drops short and I skin both palms.
    When my doctor said *Congratulations,* I heard
    Go out and live, as if it's as simple
as remembering, resuming, as if

I am not beginning again.

II.

Most people have it wrong—lactic acid
is not muscles' stored soreness

but the burning, mid-step
low-O_2 ache. Once, my fever spiked

to 106. Once, my body seized
for eight minutes and there was nothing

to be done but wait. Once, my tongue turned
black, the cells in my mouth dead, thick,

bitter, squandered. For months I ran
the shower over the sound of retching, worried

my roommates would hear. I learned
not to flinch or cringe at at-homes—

needle stab and sear—and I Ubered to the ER
19 times. I actually believed

I would save myself, come to the end
and take credit.

But more than once I thrashed,
panicked as the accelerator spun

around my body and my body
had to be restrained, my body

had to be strapped to the table—
I was so afraid

I had to be strapped to a table.

And once, I told the one I love
that I refused to die

away from the Blue Ridge. *Take me home,*
I said *If it comes to it.* Then,

Never mind.

           If illness uglies the world,
    what redeems it? If the body

        is a vessel, what then, what of mine?

III.

Just past mile twelve, I wonder
    if there's really such a thing
as *before,* as *back when,* as in
        back when I ran an 18:22 5K, *back before*

sloughed skin, layer
    after thinning layer of myself
peeled away, so easily split open. The body
        as palimpsest, dark garden, a marker

of time itself. All that space for remaking
    lit up like windows slipping by, Caeneus
the newly minted god of *ad infinitum.*

           I have learned this—the body,
    by being a body in this world is a shout: *life.*
Block after block, my Achilles strains,

    an old injury flaring, and this is what they mean—

so this is what they mean
when they say *carried*—I was carried.
    I take no credit.

IV.

I ran along the shore each night
    of my early twenties, evening's gauze stretched
    over the Atlantic. I've watched nighthawks circle
        at Split Rock, guarding eggs laid bare

among stones. And I live now
    in a place where I call cherry blossoms *usual,*
        where I dream I hold rain in tight fists, then wake
        to snow in March. It's true: *each day*

I learn more of the miraculous.
    I unlearn ageless cycles: active treatment,
    side effects, rest.
           Eighty-five years ago, almost
    to the day, Szilárd proved the atom split,

warned against the bomb then watched it drop.
   And two summers back, an orchardist was picked up
   and locked away ten years in Richland county
      for a loaded, unregistered Sig. They didn't bother

even to print his name. Each night, like a prayer, I ask
   myself—what's the difference? How will I ever know
   if I'm headed back to,   away from?

V.

Growing up, Roy and Georgia combed the yard
next door for pecans. I baled hay, picked & shelled

summer beans, put up, got hit. Raised tough—
that's what I mean. Survival carries a blade, too,

stops showing up for class junior year
except to sit state exams & graduate,

gets voted Class Jailbird & laughs
too loud. Survival loses a whole month

to a needle, wakes to a new year & runs straight
out of town with a notebook stowed

under its shirt. Survival tucks its *y'alls* in a cedar chest
& holds its breath & makes a way & cleans up & clenches all of life

& all of want between its teeth. & maybe this
Piedmont communion was my cure:

pigweed, choked tobacco leaves,
my uncle's campaign posters rotting

in the barn. Every memory of who I am
a violin playing far off and bright.

The scar on my thigh tight
as the hand to my mouth. I am an invention

of this place that haunts. What worries me most:
these days I like saying *I've become a different person*

because it's the truest thing I know.

VI.

All this, all this
    & I jog steady through
each intersection, thighs burning
       joyously.   Reveling the loop,

I sprint the last four blocks to home,
    arriving & returning
one & the same.   Can living be as simple

as a chest bound
    & free of tumors, heaving steady,
my stride counting
    one-twos down the road?

    I know I have always been
    this lucky.

My lungs catch, my vision blots
      & my hearing quits & I feel
    the body pulse—pure,
and for a moment, familiar.

Acknowledgments

These poems first appeared, sometimes in different forms, in the following journals:

> *The Adroit Journal:* "Caeneus Struck by Side Effects at a
> Late-Night 7-Eleven" and "Rough Draft as
> Caeneus Abroad"
> *The Boiler:* "Vox Populi, Vox Dei"
> *New South:* "Prayer for the Self on I-24 W"
> *Palette Poetry:* "In Response to My Mother When She
> Says Hearing Me Read My Writing's Like Hearing
> God"
> Academy of American Poets: "Self Portrait as My Mother
> Would Have It"

"Rough Draft as Caeneus Abroad" owes significant debt to my former student, S. W. M., Dr. Clarissa Pinkola Estés's *Women Who Run With the Wolves,* and a craft talk by Jos Charles at Central Washington University on April 2, 2019.

"Poem for Lactic Acid" borrows the line "Each day I learn more of the miraculous" from Lynda Hull's "Visiting Hour."

I owe so much of this book and my life to many generous souls, but we begin with the principal cast: to Lat, Amy, and Caylea Flanagan for their continued patience and faith; to Nora and Margie for their examples; and to the Sunday Beaty Road crew for their unwavering love and support from afar. Y'all have known me longest, and y'all have taught me the most.

This book owes all its wonder and luster to Melissa Crowe, Jessica Jacobs, and the folks at *Beloit Poetry Journal.* For all my firsts with you guys, my work owes a significant debt.

Many thanks to Jordan Rice and Laura Read for lending their attention and words to this project, and for their own work, which has gifted me so much.

My work would not have found a way if it weren't for the stellar cast of teachers and mentors who have helped me forge a path: Mark Cox, Thom Didato, Mary Flinn, Kathleen Graber, Michael

Keller, Bryant Mangum, Sarah Messer, and David Wojahn. And my work would simply not exist if it weren't for Sally Griffin, who saved my life in more than one way, more than once.

Thanks to my brigade of students, especially JL and SWM, who inspire me more than they know. Thank you all for trusting me with your work, too.

I have been graced with friends better than I deserve, all of whom have had a hand in this book. Thanks to Maya Jewell Zeller for the night walks and wound-talk; to Chloe Allmand, the best hype-man I could ever ask for; to Rhonda Selvig-Muller and Krislon Rhynes, queens and heroes both; to Caleb Stacy for late-night tea and for being the best, always; to Kate Doughty for being the brightest of all the bright things; to Chelsea Taylor for loving me longer than I've known how to love at all; and to Sarah Booth, for being the one I call no matter what.

Thanks to Cassandra J. Bruner, who inspires me, reassures me, and makes me braver every day. So much of this book was written because you showed me it could be done.

Thanks to RJ, wherever you are, for all those years of becoming right alongside me.

Thanks to Lina for finding me in the gutter and for the patience and points systems and playing for keeps.

And thanks to my grandfather, Ned, who gave me this strange and improbable dream so early on. (I did it after all.)